AF255990

Benoît Turquety is Associate Professor at the University of Lausanne, director of the SNF research project on Bolex and amateur cinema and of the EPIMETE/digital media epistemology research axis. He is a founding member of the *Material Archival Studies Network* and part of the *Dispositives research group*, of the *Network for Experimental Media Archaeology*, as well as the *Technology and the Humanities project*. He is the author of *Inventing Cinema: Machines, Gestures and Media History* (Amsterdam University Press, 2019). Focusing on early substandard film production, African video, or experimental poetry, his recent research aims to re-establish digital media as embedded material cultures, articulating machines, techniques, images, and sounds, modes of circulation and transmission, and networks of concepts.

Medium, Format, Configuration: The Displacements of Film

Benoît Turquety

Contents

Configurations of Film: Series Foreword

Scalable across a variety of formats and standardized in view of global circulation, the moving image has always been both an image of movement and an image on the move. Over the last three decades, digital production technologies, communication networks and distribution platforms have taken the scalability and mobility of film to a new level. Beyond the classical *dispositif* of the cinema, new forms and knowledges of cinema and film have emerged, challenging the established approaches to the study of film. The conceptual framework of index, *dispositif* and canon, which defined cinema as photochemical image technology with a privileged bond to reality, a site of public projection, and a set of works from auteurs from specific national origins, can no longer account for the current multitude of moving images and the trajectories of their global movements. The term "post-cinema condition," which was first proposed by film theorists more than a decade ago to describe the new cultural and technological order of moving images, retained an almost melancholic attachment to that which the cinema no longer was. Moving beyond such attachments, the concept of "configurations of film" aims to account for moving images in terms of their operations, forms and formats, locations and infrastructures, expanding the field of cinematic knowledges beyond the arts and the aesthetic, while retaining a focus on film as privileged site for the production of cultural meaning, for social action and for political conflict.

The series "Configurations of Film" presents pointed interventions in this field of debate by emerging and established international scholars associated with the DFG-funded Graduate Research Training Program (Graduiertenkolleg) "Konfigurationen des Films" at Goethe University Frankfurt. The contributions to the series aim to explore and expand our understanding of configurations of film in both a contemporary and historical perspective, combining film and media theory with media history to address key problems in the development of new analytical frameworks for the moving image on the move.

Introduction

Andrea Polywka, Antoine Prévost-Balga

Since September 2017, the research collective "Configurations of Film" has been dealing with questions related to film apprehended as an object that does not necessarily or primarily belong to cinema, nor should it belong exclusively to cinema studies. From this perspective, studying film requires adopting interdisciplinary approaches and investigating places other than the cinema, looking at different spaces where moving images are produced and where cinematic experiences are provided. Rather than thinking of the supposed specificities that constitute a pre-established idea of what should cinema be, what a cinematic experience should look like, and where and when it should happen, the term "configurations of film" instead recognizes the fact that, using the words by Vinzenz Hediger and Miriam de Rosa, "cinema is indeed a shape-shifting object of study." Using the term "configuration" would allow us "to apprehend cinema in its varying shapes, both as they develop over time and as they co-exist and interact with each other" (De Rosa and Hediger 2017, 17). As suggested here by Miriam De Rosa and Vinzenz Hediger, the notion of configuration could be a powerful term to think with when it comes to grasping cinema in its multiple shapes. But how to identify and apprehend, as an object of research, a configuration of film? How to deploy and put into practice this idea of configurations of film in scholarly work? Benoît Turquety's lecture "Medium, Format, Configuration: The Displacements of Film," given at the Goethe Universität on September 20, 2018, was an important contribution to understanding these questions.

Configurations and Technical Networks

Among the thin red lines that go through Benoît Turquety's works, the most constitutive one would certainly be the tendency to privilege a material and concrete approach to films and visual media objects. Initially trained as an engineer at the prestigious French École Normale Supérieur Louis-Lumière before completing his Ph.D. at the Université Paris VIII Vincennes–Saint-Denis (France) in 2005, Turquety is driven in his research by his interests and practical as well as theoretical knowledge in film techniques and technologies. His prize-winning monograph *Inventing Cinema: Machines, Gestures, and Media History* (2019) is one example where his contribution to film history and epistemology is deeply anchored in a methodology that takes as its primary objects of research the machines, their functioning structures, and the related technical documents (sketches, patents, specialized journals on photographic and cinematographic technologies, etc.). This concrete approach towards historicized and localized material objects is also clearly expressed in the way Turquety approaches the idea of "configurations of film." Indeed, he mostly discusses configurations of film in terms of "technical networks." The latter is an expression he borrowed from the French philosopher Gilbert Simondon, while referring to his work *On the Mode of Existence of Technical Objects* (1958), as well as other still untranslated works by him, such as "Psychosociologie de la Technicité" and other articles that were published in the collection *Sur La Technique* (2014). It somehow comes as no surprise that a scholar particularly interested in the machines of cinema tackles the notion of configuration via philosophers of technology such as Gilbert Simondon. Turquety has extensively shown how productive it can be to think of cinema technologies with concepts developed by Simondon. He has already done it in his aforementioned monograph *Inventing Cinema*, when he was refreshing the way we thought of cinema as an invention by firstly defining invention in a Simondonian way as a "resolution of problems," and by identifying "cinema" as a certain response given to a certain set of "problems." He does it here again this time by understanding the term "configuration" mostly as a "technical network."

Analyzing the logic behind "technical networks" especially implies taking a closer look at the material objects intervening within the networks. This is something we learn from descriptive methods such as the ones proposed by Gilbert Simondon, but also by Madeleine Akrich in her article "The De-Scription of Technical Objects" (2012), which Turquety relies on. In the case of "configuration of film" these material objects could be designated very well by the term coined by Volker Pantenburg "cinematographic objects," to which he dedicated an edited collection *Cinematographic Objects: Things and Operations* (2015). He defines "cinematographic objects" as "human and non-human actors that assemble to create a network of distributed agency," which are "stabilized in their structure" and "organized in an operational chain" by the "film image itself" (Pantenburg 2015, 13). Turquety takes two examples of "cinematographic objects" here—the Kodak Supermatic 8 processor and the VHS cassette—and elaborates on the "operational chain" constituted by these two objects in two specific contexts. In the gap between isolated technical objects and entire operational chains there are interdependencies—internal coherences as Simondon puts it—which are determined by the technicality of the objects themselves. Thus, exploring technical networks not only requires looking at the constitutive objects, but also at the way they are able (or not able) to relate to one another. Vinzenz Hediger refers to this aspect of a "configuration of film" as the "relational" one. It namely consists in studying "the ways in which the moving image relates to other elements of its configuration" (De Rosa and Hediger 2017, 18). This is precisely the "relational" aspect in Simondon's philosophy, and more specifically his philosophy of technology, which happens to be particularly efficient in the apprehension of "configurations." Indeed, Simondon not only analyzes the way technical objects dispose of their own "mode of existence," he also develops a constitutive philosophy of the relation. The broader horizon of his philosophy, which is too often reduced to a mere (but already complex) philosophy of technology, is to think of the coming-into-being of entities, their mode of existence, and their relations to their surroundings. This is an aspect of his philosophy particularly developed in his primary thesis *Individuation à la Lumière des Notions de Forme et d'Information* (2005),[1] where he tackles questions such as how individuals (being technical, mineral, vegetal, human, or animal) relate to their "associated milieu," and to what extent this relation is a constitutive part of their being.

The analysis Turquety develops in the two case studies that open his lecture on "displacements of film" is thus particularly anchored in the relational level of analysis Hediger is describing here, and more importantly in a Simondonian understanding of how certain (cinematographic) objects relate to their technical and geographical milieu. By looking successively at the Kodak Supermatic 8 processor in the context of 1970s film production in Mozambique and at the VHS cassette's role in the production and circulation of Nigerian cinema in the late 1980s, Turquety not only explores the technicality of these cinematographic objects and the way they relate, define, interact with broader technical networks, he also challenges the idealist vision of these technical networks through a close reading of two cases studies where displacements occurred. The internal coherence of a technical network is set, according to Simondon, when the material components find what he called their "key points," meaning a technical role in lines with a geographical location without which the whole functioning structure might become unstable. Simondon usually gives examples of technical objects or structures in their key points, mentioning the lighthouse on a reef, an observatory on the top of a mountain, or a bridge crossing a valley. Interesting to note is that most of the examples Simondon refers to are technical networks structured around immobile objects. The idea of displacement that Turquety introduces is thus highly challenging for the investigation of technical

---

1   While *On the Mode of Existence of Technical Objects* actually constitutes his secondary thesis.

networks that constitute configurations of film. What happens to a preexisting configuration once we dislocate it from its "key point"? Or what kind of configurations are possible if we introduce cinematographic objects somewhere else, in places that do not constitute key points? In other words, Turquety's contribution to the reflexion on "technical networks" also tackles another aspect of "configurations of film," which is the "spatial dimension of a given configuration," and more specifically in a context of displacements (De Rosa and Hediger 2017, 18).

From Medium to Format

In the industry, what allows different "technical networks" to interact, and even what allows the interaction between technical objects within a technical network, is the establishment of standards. Simondon is very specific about this point: it is not the industry that creates standardized objects, it is the standardized object that allows the industrial production to happen. Jonathan Sterne's format theory gives a relevant application for such a statement within the frame of film and media studies. As he puts it in his publication *MP3: The Meaning of a Format*, "standards assure that a format that operates on one system will operate on another" (2012, 22).

Furthermore, Sterne explains that the debate around new formats has often been mixed with revising the importance of the respective medium itself. He elaborates further: "If there is such a thing as media theory, there should also be format theory" (Sterne 2012, 7). He thus focuses on the modes of perception as well as the changing nature of these modes that demand another form of analysis. Turquety agrees with Sterne's approach when he emphasizes the distinctive vertical form of 35mm versus 16mm film, which he compares as "low" and "high" formats, or sub-standard and standard. As Sterne has pointed out, the importance of these terms came from "operational needs across media" (14). The format as an alternative notion to that of medium offers more relevance in terms of the technological and economic dimension, as Sterne and Turquety have mentioned in specific cases in both their articles.

To return to Turquety's lecture, "the main take away at the end is that the notion of medium is not precise enough to understand how technology really works," as Vinzenz Hediger pointed out during the discussion following the lecture. According to the title, the terms "Medium," "Format," and "Configuration" indicate the displacements of film in various fields and situations and in this regard Turquety is essentially focusing on the technological relevance as well as limitations of specific formats such as VHS production in Nigeria or the use of the thermic camera in the works of the Irish artist Richard Mosse. It is intriguing how Turquety on the one hand approaches the term "medium" while on the other hand distancing himself from it. This distance is already formulated in his earlier works and publications, like in his essay from 2015 "Forms of Machines, Forms of Movement," published in François Albera and Maria Tortajada's *Cine-Dispositives: Essays in Epistemology Across Media*. When he writes about the "discontinuation of film as a medium," he is referring to the problematic process of reformatting one medium into another and therefore describing modes of transformation. These modes affect not only the technological but also the terminological level and expose the non-homogeneity of film as a medium. Even though he analyzes pre-cinematic objects, like the zoetrope or phenakistiscope, his arguments are aligned with the use of the term "medium" in film theoretical debates. When he argues that "the technological analysis of machines should be confronted with their production" (Turquety 2015, 277), he presents the insufficiency of the term for this matter. Thus, it is crucial how film as a medium rather than a technological object lacks the consideration of the different formats that are introduced in his lecture. It could be mentioned here that the theoretical concept of the *dispositif* could have been an extension in his argumentation for the search for other aesthetic criteria and

to escape the characteristic homogenization of the term medium. **13**
As Michel Foucault's analysis from the 1970s has demonstrated,
the notion of dispositif supports linking heterogeneous elements
in order to study the interaction and results of their coalition
([1977] 1980, 194–195). But the question of how the dimension of
film is implicated in the concept of a technological object would
require including a more detailed examination of formats, as
Turquety has suggested.

Based on the triad of the research collective which juxtaposes
"Format(ion)," "Usage," and "Localization," Turquety offers
insightful aspects in his lecture, while positioning his argument in
the context of "configurations of film." He challenges the idea of
film objects becoming a part of technical networks and building
an alternative terminological framework consisting of three
notions "medium," "format," and "configuration." The constantly
shifting object of film in various contexts requires a more pro-
found approach that grasps the notion of film as a complex construct on several layers, as Sterne has put it in terms of technical
networks: They "are built on top of one another, like oceanic
zones or layers, and depending on the register we consider,
the political or cultural articulation of the technology may vary
widely" (2012, 16). The focus on the technological feature is crucial,
especially when Turquety elucidates that on one hand the shift
to the digital has been challenged through the use of the terms
"format," "medium" and "displacement." On the other hand, these
concepts are not valid when the contemporary form of digital
cinema is no more than a "combination of formats," as the author
further elaborates in this volume.

References

Akrich, Madeleine. 1992. "The De-Scription of Technical Objects." In *Shaping
    Technology/Building Society: Studies in Sociotechnical Change*, edited by Wiebe E.
    Bijker and John Law, 205–224. Cambridge, MA: MIT Press.
De Rosa, Miriam, and Vinzenz Hediger. 2017. "Post-what? Post-when? A Conversation
    on the 'Posts of Post-media and Post-cinema." *Cinéma & Cie International Film
    Studies Journal* 16 (26/27): 9–20.

14   Foucault, Michel. (1977) 1980. "The Confession of the Flesh." In *Power/Knowledge: Selected Interviews and Other Writings 1972–1977*, edited by Colin Gordon, 194–228. New York: Pantheon Books.

Pantenburg, Volker, ed. 2015. *Cinematographic Objects: Things and Operations*. Berlin: August Verlag.

Simondon, Gilbert. 2005. *L'Individuation à la lumière des notions de forme et d'information*. Grenoble: Millon.

—. 2014. *Sur La Technique (1953–1983)*. Paris: Presses Universitaires de France.

—. 2016. *On the Mode of Existence of Technical Objects*. Minneapolis: Univocal.

Sterne, Jonathan. 2012. *Mp3: The Meaning of a Format*. Durham, NC: Duke University Press.

Turquety, Benoît. 2015. "Forms of Machines, Forms of Movement." In *Cine-Dispositives: Essays in Epistemology Across Media*, edited by François Albera and Maria Tortajada, 275–297. Amsterdam: Amsterdam University Press.

—. 2019. *Inventing Cinema: Machines, Gestures, and Media History*. Amsterdam: Amsterdam University Press.

TECHNOLOGY

GILBERT SIMONDON

FORMAT

MEDIA

NETWORK

DIGITAL CINEMA

Medium, Format, Configuration: The Displacements of Film

Benoît Turquety

Digital cinema has replaced film. Or so the story goes. But that dominant narrative, adopted by the production industry as well as within academic circles, is based on, and consolidates, an over-homogenization of these two entities, digitally produced and chemically produced moving images. In fact, cinema was never a homogeneous "medium"; it has always been a complex layering of diverse technical and cultural practices. In contrast with *media* constructed as vast, ontologically homogeneous, non-localized systems, *formats* show material networks of interoperability and exclusions, inscribed in local specificities, and involving precise conditions for the circulation of images and sounds. Formats, institutionalized as standards, frame the "technical networks" defined by Gilbert Simondon, that unfold technical objects into economically and politically structured webs that cover the world. The attention to formats also allows us to defocus from a closed and implicitly Western conception of the "cinema" *dispositif*, to wonder for instance what happened with sound or analogue video, or what the digital transition has meant from a Nigerian perspective. Indeed, the "Nollywood" industry has had to move from analogue to digital formats—VHS, VCD, online channels, ...—producing each time new networks of circulation, and confronted each time to new problems of adaptation to regional and global environments, and to local as well as diasporic cultural ecologies.

1.   Technologies of Displacement

Within the framework of the set of exhibitions that brought together various Frankfurt art venues under the rubric *Extreme* in September 2018, the Irish artist Richard Mosse presented three photographs and one three-screen video installation at the Museum für Moderne Kunst. The four works centrally deal with the "extreme nomads" that are the title and focus of the museum's contribution to the event (MMK 2018): the photographs exhibit refugee camps, while the video, titled *Incoming*, shows "migrants"—as they are called in our public sphere—trying to survive from sinking ships to burning camps to administrative retention systems. The spectator can sense these persons' distress, their fear, their exhaustion, but can also see all the 'welcoming' infrastructures that take 'care' of them—as John Wayne might have said to Lee Marvin in an old John Ford movie—"I'll take care of you." Volunteers, doctors, firemen, policemen, fighter pilots, metallic boat cabins, survival blankets, religious icons, or cheap tents and mud, all surround these displaced persons, to finally lock them up in a seemingly endless in-between movement in a non-existing space. They left one specific place, where their history was, to reach another, where their future was supposed to be, but both are now lost and out of reach, and they are bound to blank spaces where no history can ever be inscribed.

The suspension in between that characterizes this "extreme nomadism" is given an intriguing, nightmarish visual materiality by the tools chosen by the artist. He filmed in slow motion, with a specific apparatus: a thermic camera, sensitive to levels of heat rather than to the usual visible spectrum of colors. Transcoded in a metallic black and white, the warmest objects in the shot appear as silvery white areas, whereas the colder ones come up thick grey or pitch black—or the contrary, depending on the processing choices that vary during the work. Skin colors thus keep reversing, as though they refused to connote any ethnic group anymore. They seem to reveal only heat gradients, which result from the interaction between warm life and the colder, sometimes much colder, environment. They reveal what's left of life here. Yet, the skin tone, even remediated, remains in this *dispositif* a relevant coding structure, which can't completely ignore the history of blackface or colonial carnivalesque representations, in which masks play dubious roles. Faces are nonetheless still perceptible as such in these images, and the emotions are still legible most of the time; but eyes and mouths are turned into homogeneous spots, dissolving the immediate humanity of the persons—migrants or policemen—into something suddenly problematic or fragile. The permanent slow motion adds to the nightmarish quality while dialectically compensating a little for the difficulty of having access to that humanity, by giving us time to explore the strange faces and find there what we know exists: our likeness. Sitting in a darkened corner of that Frankfurt museum gallery, warm and quiet while drowned in thick, droning sound, I watch the images produced by that thermic camera showing these people as not sharing any common space with me anymore. They are even out of the imaginary space of the usual, collective mass-media indignation. They are delocalized to a literal dystopia that appears as completely impossible to reconnect with the geographical space. Yet, it is that move to a radically disconnected, virtual space which is in itself imaginary, as the coldness of that mud is very real and precisely located.

A work about displacement, the video is also the result of a series of displacements. First, that thermic camera is of course a military *dispositif*, in fact a canonic example of these apparatuses through which "in the martial context, the human sensorium has been slowly and surely directed, mediated, and supplanted in service to the ultimate imperative of targeting" (Bousquet 2018, 12). It is used on the battlefield to identify human presence and potential enemies, whatever the visibility conditions may be. It is also used by border police to spot immigrants at long distances—the camera being able to follow automatically any moving "target." Military machines and operations are important throughout Mosse's video, and the use of that camera displaces the spectator. I would like to feel some brotherhood with these people; but the installation forces me to watch them through that very visual apparatus regularly used to kill them, allowing the sniper to isolate them from any kind of environment while its non-realist representational system helps dehumanize them. My position then becomes quite uncomfortable.

Second, the work's production process is also marked by delocalization and displacement. Shown in Frankfurt, it was made by an artist born in Ireland and now living in New York, and commissioned by two art galleries, one in London, England, the other in Melbourne, Australia. Interestingly, the video is indicated as "produced in Europe, the Middle East, and North Africa"—the Mediterranean Sea being the implicit center of this geographic constellation—but no precise localization is ever given within the work, which thus avoids any concrete political inscription within the various, heterogeneous contexts it deals with. Considering the problem from a humanist perspective,[1] the video refuses to relocate our relation with displaced persons within the specific cultural, political, historical circumstances of the different European, African, or Middle Eastern countries, cities, villages, legal systems, or forms of representation that are involved in these circulations.

On another level, it can be noted that the video's running time, within the looped installation, is rather ironically 52 minutes, the exact standard duration of a TV documentary. I am not entirely sure, though, that this will really help its worldwide diffusion. Such a three-screen HD video installation, with a 7.3 surround sound[2] whose aesthetics are largely based on physical power, of

1   As claimed by the artist on his website (Mosse 2017).
2   As indicated by the museum; the artist's website indicates 7.1 surround sound.

course eludes all the dominant distribution channels: its technical format prevents its diffusion in any place other than an art gallery or museum. The problem could be circumvented by creating a one-screen stereo version, in the way Harun Farocki sometimes did with works he reformatted from one medium to another. This change of format indeed means a complete transformation of the work itself. In any case, the complexity of the wide diffusion of *Incoming* is in fact not a problem, as it belongs to an economy of art that is based on the tension between the desired wide circulation of the name of the artist and the organized scarcity of the artefacts, which must remain sellable items. This entails restricted access. The artwork must participate in the flow of global media products, while resisting its inner logic of dissemination and multiplication. This is organized by legal *dispositifs* such as copyright, but as we all know these are only relatively efficient, and can quite easily be bypassed, with only little inner moral conflict; restrictions, or "exclusions" as Madeleine Akrich and others have formulated (Akrich 1992, 209, 223), are also and more safely inscribed technically within the formats of the pieces. In a Latourian logic, the control of the work's value on the art market is thus delegated to a technical artefact: the format.

In fact, this case should also lead us to distinguish between several types of formats, or rather to consider each media production as a precise combination of various formats: those used during the production process, and those of the final object, this object including the artefact and its performance. *Incoming* was shot with a single-lens military device, in an unspecified source format. The video signal is finally coded in HD. The end element synchronizes three HD signals, together with 10-channel sound. Again, this format requires a very precise apparatus to be seen and heard as it should. The perceptual result for the spectator depends on all these factors—as well as the shape of the room, etc.

Formats are always already heterogeneous objects. Each format combination might in fact correspond to a specific

media *configuration*, whose coherence as such might be more
meaningful than the level of the medium itself. Jonathan Sterne
has argued for the move "from mediality to formats" and the
foundation of a "format theory." To him, "*Format* denotes a whole
range of decisions that affect the look, feel, experience, and
workings of a medium. It also names a set of rules according
to which a technology can operate" (2012, 7). Sterne is centrally
interested in the perceptual implications of formats, which won't
be my main focus. The set of rules refers to another level: that of
protocols and standards that guarantee the readability and circulation of the files. The technology operates when the work can
be played not only by my own machines, but also by the machines
of all the people with which I wish to share the listening or
viewing experience. Sterne's perspective is oriented by his object,
the MP3 sound format, and thus privileges wide, informal circulation, even piracy. Mosse's situation in the art world is deeply different, and formats there involve circulation *control* rather than
viral propagation.

My claim here will be that formats in fact constitute a rather
rigid geopolitical structure that connects perceptual aspects
with a complex system of global media currents and cultural
hierarchies. From an art historical perspective, David Summers
has also used the notion of format: "The encounter of an
observer with a virtual space, before it is an encounter with a
vast panorama or a furious battle, takes place before a culturally
specific *format*—a screen, polyptych or book, for example—in
personal and social space" (2003, 44, emphasis in original).
Format here describes the material shape of the artwork, but the
example of the canvas then analyzed by Summers shows that the
notion not only refers to scale or support matter, but also to port-
ability, sellability, and the various local practices that condition
the spectator's reception as well as the work's status and modes
of circulation. Formats regulate the artworks' embodiment
and their embeddedness; they transcode cultural, technical,
economic, and ecological historicity into concrete objects and

networks. For Summers, formats constitute the junction between the virtual space of the image considered as what Wiesing would call "artificial presence" (2010) and the social space of art as a *dispositif*. David Joselit has insisted on the cross-linking potential of formats: "Formats are dynamic mechanisms for aggregating content.… formats are nodal connections and differential fields; they channel an unpredictable array of ephemeral currents and charges" (2013, 55). To him, this perspective on contemporary art forms and diffusion modes entails that "we must discard the concept of *medium* (along with its mirror image, the postmedium)," to "expand the definition of art to embrace heterogeneous configurations of relationships or links—what the French artist Pierre Huyghe "has called 'a dynamic chain that passes through different formats'" (2). I will also explore here the tension between the concepts of *media* and *formats*, and argue that a relevant description of local, always heterogeneous *configurations* of film must rely on the level of *format* rather than on that of the *medium*. But I will argue moreover that if formats do channel the global currents of media flow, they do so as solid, obdurate entities. Formats were partly conceived to make the array of currents and charges less ephemeral and more predictable. They are what's left of stability in today's largescale media dissemination. As we will see, formats certainly got reconfigured by the turn from analogue to digital technologies, but the concept and the functions were maintained—or maybe they were reconstructed.

In order to describe this more precisely, I would like to present two case studies, each connected to a specific time and place. These will show that media are concretely framed. Formats lie at the interface between production and diffusion, between the aesthetic and the economic, between the perceptual and the geopolitical. Media technologies inscribe modes of representation, but simultaneously pertain to the logics of the industrialized technical object. Showing how formats relate to Gilbert Simondon's notion of "technical networks" will then allow me to establish the interdependences and interferences

between the object as tool and the object as a node of networks.
If *network* is an important notion in our disciplines, partly thanks
to Bruno Latour's contributions, Simondon's perspective on the
concept will remain central here as it defocuses from the single
object while maintaining its materiality, and furthermore directly
involves a concrete geography of circulations. Technical networks
are, in Simondon, what reveal technical objects as geopolitically
and environmentally charged worldwide machineries. Standardization, as the process of institutionalization of formats into
standards, is an essential moment: as guaranteeing the viability
of production and distribution networks it is the condition of possibility for the presence of media products in cultures. It involves
a change of scale, moving from the singularity of the prototype or
of the original handcrafted work to a population of similar copies,
interchangeable or interoperable—or not. Standards have, I will
argue, structured the global mediascape into separate networks
whose frontiers further the colonial history deep into our supposed free-trade world. As organizing the displacements of works
and objects on wide scales, standardized formats also constitute
the relevant framework for the apprehension of the environmental impact of media technologies.

The first case study is a classic though complex instance of
technology transfer within media history. The co-founder of
Actor-Network Theory Madeleine Akrich has shown, in "The
De-Scription of Technical Objects," the interest of "follow[ing
a] device as it moves into countries that are culturally or his-
torically distant from its place of origins" (1992, 211). These displacements, de-stabilizing both objects and users, allow us to
observe the "reinventing and reshaping of technical objects in
use" (212). They thus reveal the extent to which technics, linking
practices with technologies, are place-dependent. From a post-
phenomenological perspective, Don Ihde has also proposed that
technology transfers be used as privileged objects for a "cultural
hermeneutics" of technology (1990, 124), a move that could lead
to the understanding of "neocolonialism as the failure of transfer"

(131)—though I would argue that neocolonialism can also appear in the shape of quite successful transfers. Technological transfers are indeed highly interesting in that they constitute a practice that crosses the line between colonial and postcolonial eras, emerging from the first and perpetuating into the second, with ideological grounds that are only partly dissimilar.

2. Formats and the Strategies of Independence (Mozambique, 1978)

We are in Maputo, capital city of the Democratic Republic of Mozambique, in the summer of 1978. The country has only been independent for three years, some fifteen years later than the vast majority of African countries. Immediately after the declaration of independence, socialist leader Samora Machel made major decisions concerning cinema. Refusing the typical African situation of having the local theaters flooded with films coming from the United States, Hong Kong, or India, Machel decided to "decolonize film distribution," and so nationalized the entire Mozambican film distribution system. In November 1975, he created the National Film Institute, whose aim was not only to produce films but to create and organize a complete and viable cinema in the country. For now, there was neither technical infrastructure nor trained filmmakers, so a transition phase was organized in which the money coming from the theaters funded the shooting of films by guest filmmakers, coming from other socialist countries or from international leftist circles.[3] The films were shown in the country, but also went outside, to raise funds. Notably, 16mm prints circulated within the network of US university film clubs—with help and support from friends like Ethiopian filmmaker Haile Gerima—which were quite open to supporting a young Marxist country in Africa. In three years, Mozambique had managed to build the facilities and buy the equipment that

3   On this situation, see Diawara 1992, 88–103.

would allow them to produce 16mm and 35mm black-and-white
film independently, and to gather a team of trained filmmakers.
In 1978, internationally renowned filmmaker Ruy Guerra, who was
born in Mozambique but had lived and worked in Brazil, came
back from exile to chair the Film Institute. They started the production of a weekly series of ten-minute political newsreels titled
Kuxa Kanema. For each episode, eight 35mm prints were made, to
be exhibited in the urban movie theaters. But they also wanted to
show the films in rural areas, where no theaters existed. Political
solidarity solved the problem: the USSR gave the new brother-
country a set of mobile projection units, vans equipped with
16mm sound projectors and electric generators, which would
bring the cinema everywhere the words of Samora Machel would
need to be heard.

Help not only came from the Soviet Union, since the birth of a
new nation, representing the potential opening of a new market
or new economic partnerships, also attracted friendly and "dis-
interested" support from countries which shared few obvious
principles with the young republic. From France, for instance.
During the 1970s, filmmaker and ethnologist Jean Rouch had
developed a growing interest for the format introduced by
Eastman Kodak in 1965, Super 8 film. It was partly connected
with the pedagogical part of his career, as he had created a
visual anthropology diploma at Nanterre University, and wanted
students to make films. 16mm would be too expensive; and as the
early 1970s saw the development of high-grade Super 8 with sync
sound, Rouch decided to use the new format as an experimental
pedagogical opportunity. After a first trip to Mozambique in 1977,
he proposed expanding the idea to create a "Super 8 workshop"
within the University of Maputo. Three "experts" were sent from
Paris together with ten complete sets of Super 8 equipment,
including cameras, editors, projectors, microphones, etc.—equipment that was paid for by the French Ministry of Foreign Affairs
as part of a "cooperation" program with the new country. The

 workshop gathered about twenty Mozambican students for three months in the summer of 1978.[4]

Beyond the workshop itself, Rouch's explicit aim was to establish the possibility of an entirely autonomous film production in African countries. In this context, his choice of the Super 8 format was connected with several crucial aspects. First, the equipment, conceived for Western amateur filmmakers, was quite cheap. As Rouch himself noted (Rouch 1982, 21–22; Oudart and Terres 1979, 54–59), it was not that simple though, because this orientation towards amateurs also implied that some of the technical characteristics (lenses, microphones, etc.) were not up to basic standards. Some had to be replaced by more expensive elements. Second, the equipment could be used after only a short training course, and did not require the long education involved with "professional" machines. So everyone could learn to make films. Third, Super 8 machines could be repaired by local technicians. This was again not that simple, as some spare parts were harder to get, but cameras and projectors being basically mechanical apparatuses, solutions could probably be found. The fourth reason had to do with a 1975 innovation which was of major historical importance for Rouch: the introduction of the Kodak Supermatic 8 Processor, an autonomous film lab the size of an office printer and able to process Super 8 color film automatically, with sound should it be desired. This was decisive, because it suddenly uncovered the possibility of an entirely autonomous local film production, which would become completely independent from European technical facilities. It would also allow for films to be shot in the morning, processed and edited in the afternoon, and shown to the people in the evening, even in distant villages.

There remained problems though, as for instance Super 8, like all amateur film systems, is a reversal format, which means that

---

4   The workshops are described in a report that can be found in the INA archives at the Bibliothèque nationale de France (Alencar et al. 1979).

there is only one fragile original of each film, with no negative and no possibility of duplicating prints. That was not a problem for Rouch at the beginning, as he thought these films should be "postcards," aimed at creating a social process of interaction and self-representation. These postcards weren't thought in terms of long-term use and preservation. But as the films proved more important than originally assumed, the problem became critical, and Rouch had to commission the French company Beaulieu to make a special printer that could duplicate reversal prints (Rouch 1982, 25). That *was* expensive.

Another Western filmmaker was in Maputo in the summer of 1978. Jean-Luc Godard and his company Sonimage had indeed signed a two-year contract with the Mozambican government for the creation of a national television in the country. Godard and a small team came for two weeks at the end of August, also with equipment that would remain there. Aiming at tele-vision production, Godard opted for video: he brought Sony and Hitachi cameras, Nivico (JVC) recorders, etc. But the technological transfer immediately appeared more complicated than expected. He wrote the day after his arrival:

> Right away in the middle of practice. The little black and white Sony is unable to read the archives it has itself recorded of the armed struggle and early independence. Besides, it complies with US standards, and that alone would be a problem should we want to edit its images with those of today or tomorrow.... The terrible feeling of a foreign power imposing on the national its knowledge and its technology already looms in the room. (1979, 82)[5]

Video electronic equipment was not adapted to the African physical environment—heat, humidity, etc. Breakdowns were frequent and not easy to repair, given the local technicians' lack of familiarity with electronics at the time, and the scarcity of

5   Unless otherwise noted, all translations are mine.

spare parts that had to come from faraway countries. Godard also discovered in the next few days that video was not adapted to African lights and contrasts, or to the Mozambican cultural color palette: what was shot at the local market was utterly disappointing. Moreover, the video team had to deal with the geography of video formats. The cameras were Japanese, and that country shares the US NTSC color video format. At that time, the Mozambique television institution was still debating whether they would choose the PAL standard—a German, 576-line format—or the SECAM one—a 625-line format created in France. That decision was of critical importance, as it would integrate the country within specific networks of compatibilities and incompatibilities. They would allow for the circulation of equip-ment and programs along different lines, and so indeed create different commercial and ideological partnerships. PAL covered most of Western Europe, Northern and Eastern Africa—including Mozambique's closest neighbors—and Asia. SECAM covered France and Francophone Africa, but also the USSR and its closest allies, which was an important argument. NTSC, centered on the American capitalist and imperialist enemy, was out of the ques-tion. So the historic images produced by the Sony machine would remain impossible to integrate within future television programs, even if the apparatus could finally be made to work again…

These three groups—the National Institute, the Super 8 group, and the television project—soon came into conflict with one another. Guerra for instance attacked Rouch, claiming that Super 8 condemned Mozambique to an aesthetically poor representation, and prevented the country from establishing a real professional film industry. Rouch answered that 35 or even 16mm were too expensive to be sustainable in the African con-text, and denoted nothing but a complex of inferiority towards Western film production. As for Jean-Luc Godard, he just left.

3.   Low Formats, High Standards (Nigeria and the Video Industry)

The second situation I would like to present has us move to Lagos, Nigeria, some twenty to thirty years later. The city has become the center of what has come to be recognized as the second largest film production industry in the world, right after Mumbai and far above Hollywood. This recognition took several years—and is still problematic—mainly because that film production was never made on film: it has always been a video-based industry. As Afolabi Adesanya (2000), Jonathan Haynes (2016), Onookome Okome (2010), and others have shown, the factors for the sudden emergence, rapid growth, and specific form of that industry at the beginning of the 1990s are quite complex, including aspects of media history—cinema, television, theater, etc.—but also of cultural, military, and economic history. For instance, the Structural Adjustment Programme implemented in Nigeria in 1986, under the auspices of the World Bank and International Monetary Fund, played an important role in its constitution, as the devaluation of the naira made it virtually impossible to produce celluloid film. Indeed, film stock production as well as chemical processing and postproduction facilities were non-existent in the country, which implied commercial exchanges with London that quickly became impossible due to the extremely low value of Nigerian money.

But such an industry cannot be understood solely from its economic data. Its products must be taken into account. As with the art installation I have described, the technical decisions are systematically related to an economic, political, or environmental context, as well as to formal characteristics. All these delineate the circulation of the work. Let's take for instance a 2010 film that is at the same time paradigmatic and a bit exceptional in the "Nollywood" landscape: *My Soul Mate*, written and directed by Michael Jaja. The main character, Winnie, is played by the star Mercy Johnson. At the beginning of the film, she announces that she is pregnant to her boyfriend, who is obviously not very interested in fatherhood—he is in fact already with another woman, and simply throws her out. Realizing her situation, Winnie, in tears, confides her problem to her best friend Jenny, who tries to help her find a practical solution. But Winnie decides to run away, and stay away until she has her child. A long time later, we find Winnie again, who is now a successful woman. But she must go in search of her lost child.

The themes, the acting style, the protracted exchange of glances at the end of the most intense scenes, seem to participate in the wide global tradition of melodrama, and particularly of tele-novelas—a major reference point for Nollywood production (Haynes 2016, 89–91; Ogundele 2000). In fact, during the dialogue with her friend Jenny, Winnie seems willing to embody melodrama itself, confronted with the common sense and pragmatic politics of the Real as personified by Jenny. Jenny knows what "strong characters do," she says; but Winnie will show her that she is one, even if within another "philosophy": that of melodrama. Running away is not a realistic solution; but it is a dramatic one. These two logics being incompatible, the final shot/reverse shot, with its excessive duration and silent, stunned faces, reveals a blocked situation. This provokes the implosion of the film's formal structure. After what will be revealed as an ellipsis of several years, Winnie suddenly addresses the spectator directly, in a monologue mixing guilt, pride, and self-hatred, ending in a quite majestic final tear rolling down her cheek as she invites the spectator to follow her and witness the rest of the tale. From that moment on, Winnie keeps talking to the spectator regularly throughout the film. These asides, happening some-times suddenly in the middle of a collective fictional scene, alter the strong linearity of the melodramatic structure. That linear basis is further broken up by the many physical transformations undergone by Mercy Johnson through the film, as Winnie's life takes many different turns, from her pregnancy and struggle for financial independence, up to the moment when, after many hardships, she finds her child again, together with the love of the one decent man she meets, played by famous Ghanaian actor Van Vicker. The film thus becomes a fragmented tribute to the versatility of Mercy Johnson's talent, as much as a monument of gender politics. Besides, the tension between linearity and fragmentation is inscribed in a large part of Nollywood production. The films are long—typically two parts of 3 hours each, possibly doubled by a sequel of a similar duration—and caught between the "film" model on the one hand, which was never abandoned, if only on the distribution level, and the "television series" model on the other.

That film was obviously shot in digital, but that was not how it all started, even though celluloid was never part of that history. Nollywood has dated its birth with the production in 1992 of *Living in Bondage*, produced by an Igbo electronics dealer, Kenneth Nnebue, and directed by Chris Obu Rapi. It was shot in the S-VHS format, and sold on VHS cassette tapes—Jonathan Haynes noting that "the cassette's full-color jacket and cellophane wrapper" was of major importance, as it "made it look comparable to an imported Hollywood film" (2016, 14). Spoken in Igbo and subtitled in English, the film was a huge success, and circulated throughout the country by "the same national distribution system that carried Hollywood and Bollywood films." Many followers immediately started producing other films according to the same model, first in Igbo then soon in Yoruba, and in English—which are now the dominant languages. The model also spread to many other African countries, on various scales: Ghana—the second most important industry—, Tanzania, Kenya, Burkina Faso, Uganda, the Democratic Republic of Congo, or Ethiopia[6]…

The VHS cassette was a cheap technology. As a shooting format, S-VHS had many constraints that were, again, hardly compatible

6   See the texts by Tunde Oladunjoye, Don Pedro Obaseki, Ibbo Daddy Abdoulaye, Franck Baku Fuita and Godefroid Bwiti Lumisa, Ogova Ondego, in Barrot 2005, 71–122.

 with African locations—Africa was of course far from the format and machine designers' minds, as it was no market at all, not even an emergent one. Neocolonialism can also take the shape of market risk evaluation. Particularly, the very low exposure latitude of VHS almost forced filmmakers to film indoors with closed curtains, fleeing the high contrasts of bright sunlight. But filmmakers adapted to the format. They displaced it to a geographical space it was not conceived for, but also to uses—making a feature film—that the designers of the format hadn't really considered. VHS was way below broadcast standards, either in terms of contrast, colors, or definition, and would be refused by any television; it was made for little more than home movies. But as Madeleine Akrich wrote, the understanding of a technical object cannot rely only on the designer's point of view—nor, for that matter, on the user's. "Instead we have to go back and forth continually between the designer and the user, between the designer's projected user and the real user, between *the world inscribed in the object and the world described by its displacement*" (1992, 208–209, emphasis in the original).

Here, the concrete displacement of the VHS camcorder from the global North to Nigeria provoked a massive displacement of the uses and practices it was involved in, of the types of people that used it, of their aims, expectations, and gestures. To Sony's "projected user," conceived as a wealthy blue-eyed father filming his children playing on the beach during the holidays, Nigerian filmmakers opposed a *projected machine* turning the VHS camcorder into a fantasized 35mm Technicolor camera, or at least a professional, broadcast TV camera, able to lay the foundations for a prosperous film industry, a star system, etc. Nollywood VHS became the displacement of Hollywood film.

If that displacement finally worked, it is also because if VHS was unheard of as a shooting format, it could on the other hand dispose of a fantastic distribution *network*, already in place and quite easy to access, in which it would fit immediately—that of Hollywood and Bollywood imported movies. As Haynes noted, there were more VCRs in Nigeria than in any other African country at the time (2016, 11); but the relative cheapness and easy accessibility of VHS machines ensured that video cassettes could be played in many places around the world. They could also almost as easily be copied, either with two simple VCRs or with dedicated systems. From the start, piracy ensured that the circulation of these films was much wider than the already important number of copies officially sold (Lobato 2012, 55–67). Even as far as the Caribbean island of Saint-Lucia, "Nigerian video films and their counterpart industry in Ghana are by far the most popular bootleg DVDs sold on this sidewalk market in a city where almost all media has been pirated from its original version" (Okome 2010, 30).

Piracy also meant that people were more often than not watching second or third—or more—generation copies (Larkin 2004). This generated a singular aesthetics, that had to do with the specificities of the format but also with local media practices, in particular the visual and sound consequences of multiple copying: blurry contours, lines crossing the image, sudden jumps, etc. Noisy VHS is the aesthetic matter of early Nollywood, not really a format in the strict, technical sense, but quite close to certain perceptual qualities of formats as described by Jonathan Sterne in the MP3 case.

Nollywood VHS cassettes could technically use that pre-existing distribution network, but they also needed to integrate its discursive modes, particularly jackets. But the VHS format had other implications. It could not be projected in the movie theaters of the global North. No commercial theater, no film archive, no festival, had VHS projectors—except maybe in their meeting room. Nollywood analogue video production was technically maintained underneath the radars of European symbolic legitimation. And in fact, it seemed to show little interest. It has sometimes been argued that movements like Cinema Novo in Brazil were in a sort of contradiction, claiming cultural independence from the powerful so-called "developed" former colonizing countries, while

36   still searching for the approval of Italian, French, or Canadian festivals, journals, and critics. There is no such contradiction in the Nollywood case. It lived and thrived entirely outside of that system—as, for that matter, it also developed without or even against the reticence of the local cultural elite. Nollywood films do not care about Western spectators. *My Soulmate* is totally indifferent to me.

But VHS, of course, disappeared. The film production in Lagos moved to digital, like everywhere else in a way. As Haynes explains, "around 2000, video compact discs (VCDs) were introduced and gradually became the standard medium. (VCDs are inferior in quality to DVDs but cheaper to produce; used in wealthier countries for data storage, they are a medium for films in the Far East as well as Africa)" (2016, 16). Presenting 352 pixel wide images in the PAL format—that is, about the quarter in size of the usual TV screen—VCDs have the other particularity of having no copy protection system—which preserved an essential feature of the Nollywood ecology.

In parallel with the turn to VCDs, the industry also developed distribution through online channels and streaming platforms. This permitted the films to reach certain types of audience more easily, notably the African diasporas. As in other fields concerned with digital diffusion, new economies had to be invented. For instance, *My Soulmate* was for a while available on YouTube, as a "loss leader" for one of the most important Nollywood diffusion websites, irokotv.com. But at the middle of the film, there suddenly seemed to be a problem: the video file seemed to get corrupt, and the image dissolved into blocks of color pixels. After a fade to black, Mercy Johnson herself appeared for a short ad, asking the spectator to subscribe to irokotv... of course, this commercial integrated within the YouTube version of the film, introduced by a simulated file defect problem, was all the more wonderful that in it, Mercy Johnson herself, with yet another different dress and yet another different hairdo, addressed the spectator directly... like she constantly does in the rest of the film!

This is a typical case of the distribution process leaving its imprint on the work itself. It was here more visible than in other, more implicit cases, but it can be argued that this sort of feedback from the economic into the formal or the perceptual is systematic. In the traditional 35mm distribution system, the marks put by projectionists at the end of each reel to allow for continuous projection are another example of such a feedback.

4. From Media to Formats: Material Structures of the Global Media Flow

These two situations—early independent Mozambique and post-structural adjustment Nigeria—are of course quite different, being some twenty years and five thousand kilometers away from each other. But the displacements at work in each case may help us clarify our perspectives on the notions at stake here.

First, it appears quite clearly that to describe these phenomena, *medium* is too wide a notion. What structures these situations is more precise, and more obdurate in its materiality. In Mozambique, the strongest conflict appeared not between cinema and television, but between 35 and 16mm black-and-white film on the one hand, and color Super 8 film on the other. Film in general, or cinema as a medium, does not constitute a coherent whole here, it does not represent a relevant level for analysis. The project of the National Film Institute and that of the Super 8 group have common points, but they cannot be homogenized under the vast notion of *medium*, as their contradictions are too important regarding their inscription within the local space and culture. For the complexity of that inscription to be recognized, we need to approach these entities with notions than can describe their material dimension, for it is at this concrete level that the geographical interaction plays the greatest part.

In fact, the notion of *medium* is not only too wide and abstract; it may also have only limited relevance. The forms of practices and production that we need to describe here are very capable of crossing traditional media borders. Nollywood history has moved between television, live traveling theater of the Yoruba tradition, itinerant projections of filmed theater (filmed on reversal 16mm stock), low grade analogue video, and various digital forms. These transformations do have important implications, in terms of costs, modes of circulation, or aesthetic experience. But the continuity is also striking. And we cannot assume that changes of media are the most important ones. As Sterne wrote: "Changes of format can be at least as significant to consider as changes *of* or *across* media" (2012, 16, emphasis in the original). For instance, the move from VHS to VCDs seems to imply little change either in terms of shooting conditions or in terms of distribution systems and networks. It could be argued that the turn from physical media to "immaterial" channels of diffusion on the internet, even if it remains strictly within the digital reign, involves greater modifications in the system as a whole than the shift from analogue to digital as such.

What I think both these situations reveal is how strongly *formats* structure the mediascape—or should we say, each geographically specific mediascape.[7] This relation to geography can be directly inscribed on a first, spatial level of structure. NTSC, PAL, and SECAM divided the world into areas that echoed economic and political alliances. But this level of immediate partnership was complicated by other criteria, which could bring into play industrial rivalry, colonial history, and linguistic, geographical, or cultural proximity. Later, DVD and Blu-ray region codes exhibited different geographies, with corresponding copyright policies. Video distribution formats, as infrastructures[8], thus extend longer histories, notably the colonial one, into the concrete technical organization of contemporary media flows.

7   On the importance of formats in media studies, see for instance Wasson 2015.

8   This notion is at the center of a growing literature. See for instance Parks and Starosielski 2015.

But formats also involve a vertical structure, which is super-imposed over the spatial one. 35mm film is a *high* format, whereas 16mm is a *low* one, qualified as *substandard*—and Super 8 an even lower one. These distinctions involve concrete differences in use and circulation, both in social and economic terms: 35mm is a professional format, Super 8 is an amateur one. Super 8 cameras are consumer technology; their design should appeal to a large public, and they should not be too expensive. 35mm cameras are rented and not bought; as professional tools they have to be reliable and adaptable to expert users and specific projects. 16mm has hybrid characteristics: invented as an amateur format, it became a professional one mostly after the Second World War. It remained favored by ambitious, rich, or expert amateurs and filmmakers at the margin of the industry, particularly when it was still considered as a viable distribution format. In the digital, HD is explicitly *high*, SD is supposed to be "standard," but that means *low*—like at Starbucks Coffee, where "tall" actually means "small." "High" seems to rely on technical and aesthetic criteria: a high "quality" image, with high definition, high exposure latitude, etc. In fact, this qualification is superficially technical—or aesthetic—and deeply ideological. This notion of "quality" actually refers to the quantity of information that the medium is supposed to be able to carry; it thus comes from information theory, and cannot be transferred into the aesthetic field without major assumptions that can hardly be justified.

That vertical structure is essential, and has implications beyond the question of cultural value. Working in the "high" film industry involves more expensive equipment, and implies specific conditions, regulated by trade unions and collective labor agreements. High formats mean higher salaries. That hasn't changed much from celluloid to digital.

On the distribution side, the problem is at least as important—and that is arguably the point where the digital turn has had the deepest impact on film history. The shift to digital means of distribution, whether in the theaters or outside, has technically blurred lines that were well-established, and that were crucial to the whole system of regulating and funding the film industry. In the analogue world, things were quite clear cut. All movie theaters in the world could project a universally standard object: the 35mm print, with 4 perforations on each side of the frame, a soundtrack with a specific form and place on the celluloid strip, etc. Some could also project 16mm, but nothing else. You could not be called a "cinema" if you couldn't project 35mm film; but if you could, you were—at least in most Western countries—eligible for public subsidies, had access to official prints and marketing materials, etc. If you only had a beamer, you obviously didn't. Most film clubs or educational environments only had 16mm projectors: this restricted their screening capacity to specific, educational films, or *low* versions of film classics. Format constraints kept them outside of the commercial network, which allowed them to develop a specific aesthetic and political position, but was also in fact the condition for their survival. It kept them under the radar of Hollywood's financial interest. But the digital blurred this technical, material distinction. The difference between a "film" projector and a beamer wouldn't be that clear anymore. Before, there was no way a VHS cassette could be played in a traditional cinema. But now, movie theaters can play "films" shot with smartphones, and such a prestigious institution as the Deutsches Filmmuseum in Frankfurt recently presented Otto Preminger's *The Cardinal* from a Blu-ray. This softening of the technical edges of distribution formats has made it possible for festivals like the Nollywood Week in Paris to exist.

In fact, the sudden decrease in the rigidity of the vertical structure inscribed in formats has played a central role in the very visibility of the Nigerian video industry on the global level. Published in 2009, the 2006 Unesco survey of feature film production around the world revealed an astonishing situation: "Nigeria surpasses Hollywood as the world's second largest film producer." Before the year 2000, many critics and historians could claim that there was no such thing as film production in Nigeria.

But in 2006, films were massively made in digital formats, be it in Hollywood or in Lagos. So the 872 films made in Nigeria that would have counted "only" as video a few years before, couldn't be ignored anymore, and the country's feature film production, which before was estimated at about zero, suddenly turned out to be more important than that of the US. In 2006 though, Nigeria had been producing approximately that number of films for more than ten years.

But that confusion brought within the structure of the global media ecology by the digital turn was a major problem for some of its most powerful actors. It badly needed to be reinstalled, so that the circulation of money and productions could be maintained within a similar frame to what the film industry had patiently constructed. There still needed to be "cinema" as opposed to "video-projection," "movie theaters" with "high" standards as opposed to temporarily arranged municipal halls, classrooms, or "low" video parlors. And that needed to be inscribed on a technical level, delegated to technical artefacts, as this would be the only actually controllable and enforceable materialization of the structure. It would moreover generate its own flow of money, theater owners having to buy the required (expensive) equipment. So the industry established the "D-cinema" *standard*, aimed at precisely that: in order to continue to be called a "cinema" even with only an electronic projector, each screening room had to comply with precise technical specifications. These were formulated in a series of texts produced between 2005 and 2012 by Digital Cinema Initiatives, LLC, an entity created by seven Western motion picture studios: Disney, Fox, Metro-Goldwyn-Mayer, Paramount Pictures, Sony Pictures Entertainment, Universal Studios, and Warner Bros Studios. They in fact defined what cinema was in the digital era. This Digital Cinema standard was created as a combination of formats: the image should be 2K or 4K, meaning either 2048 or 4096 pixels wide; there should be 24 or 48 frames per second; the image compression should be JPEG 2000, with one TIFF file per frame, and no inter-image compression; color should be coded in 12 bits per color in an X'Y'Z' color space; sound should appear as uncompressed WAV/PCM files; etc. All would be encapsulated in a Digital Cinema Package, a DCP, the most important part of the format specifications concerning in fact not the sensual aspects of the performance, but the encryption and protection of the data against copying and piracy (DCI 2018).

The explicit aim of all these technical requirements was aesthetic, and centered on the spectator. It was to ensure that: "The Digital Cinema system shall have the capability to present a theatrical experience that is better than what one could achieve now with a traditional 35mm Answer print" (DCI 2018, 15). The perceptual aspect was obviously central, but in fact, the standard was also made to re-establish the continuity between the new and his-torical *high* formats, to preserve the hierarchy as such. Standards indeed aim at the stabilization of the system—which should be reassuring to the right people. After the first announcements in the *SMPTE Motion Imaging Journal* the year before (DCI 2004), that goal was formulated by the DCI as early as their first press release in 2005: "These specifications should provide a common ground to spur innovation and encourage many more players who were previously resistant to invest capital in technology that may or may not be viable" (DCI 2005).

The "Digital Cinema" standard had the desired effect. The recon-struction of the format hierarchy was not as rigid and firm as it used to be, but it could do with a bit of flexibility. In any case, the most important aspects of the old structure were rein-forced. *Cinema* was saved. Most interestingly, the 2013 Unesco survey saw the number of feature films produced in the world hit a record high (UIS 2016b). India was still first, with 1,724 films produced during the year, mostly in digital. Then came the US (738 films), China (638), Japan (591) and France (270).[9] After that top list, a sentence specified that "it is important to note that

9   These data are also presented and analyzed in UIS 2016a.

Nigeria is not included in the analysis because most 'Nollywood' feature films are produced in video format" (UIS 2016b). So the confusion brought by the digital turn had now been "taken care of": the redefinition of a "Digital Cinema" through the construction of a specific technical standard had Nigerian production get back to the status of "low" video. The Western-defined "Digital Cinema" standard here avowed its neo-colonial dimension, with the complicity of an institution that should precisely struggle against this: the UNESCO.

5. Formats, Standards, and Technical Networks

In fact, if formats do have this power to structure the field, it is inasmuch as they are established and recognized as norms and standards. Both these terms are in fact quite problematic concepts, all the more so in that their meaning is ambiguous, as they carry heavy and partly divergent political connotations. On a basic level, they are intrinsically linked with the industrial phase of a technical object. As Gilbert Simondon has argued, the object as such only makes for a coherent unit, a complete and autonomous individual, in the case of craftsmanship or of the prototype. As soon as some dimension of industrial *concretization* is involved, the object loses its initial coherence. As he wrote in 1961: "The totality isn't at the level of the object anymore, as it was in the artisanal phase: it *condenses* in the spare part and *expands* in a huge network of distribution of these parts all around the globe" (2014, 69).

The industrial technical object has thus lost its autonomy: it appears as an aggregate of parts that must be replaceable, and simultaneously as one knot of a vast network that incorporates it. A car is not autonomous, it is "an element of a technical complex [*ensemble*] constituted by the network of roads [and road signs], by the network of gas stations, by the network of posts

 distributing spare parts and adjusting the necessary settings"
(Simondon 2014, 309).

A technical object can in fact only be conceived as a section of
networks, which include material things, like parts but also repair
tools, as well as immaterial ones, like know-how. In the absence
of the required networks, whether for historical or geographical
reasons, the object becomes unusable. It is a definition of
obsolescence. A celluloid film camera requires labs to process
the films, a transportation system able to take charge of the rolls,
the chemical knowledge and products necessary for the making
of the celluloid, of the emulsion, and for their later processing,
etc. Without these external elements, a Bolex camera is not a
technical object anymore; it is just a museum piece. It becomes
useless, and its coherence ungraspable. The reasons for the
place, form, and size of the crank on the machine's side can only
be understood while making it work. Its technicality conditions
the way it relates with its environment, the gestures and modes
of expertise it requires, etc. Questioning a camera in terms of its
technicality implies inscribing it in a geography.

In Simondon's terms,

> Technicality is a mode of being that can only fully and per-
> manently exist as a network, in a temporal as well as a
> spatial way. Temporal reticulation is made with reworkings of
> the object in which it is updated, renovated, renewed in the
> very conditions of its first making. Spatial reticulation con-
> sists in the fact that technicality cannot be contained within
> one single object; an object is technical only if it operates
> in relation with other objects, in a network where it takes
> the meaning of a key point; in itself and as object, it only
> possesses virtual elements of technicality that materialize
> in the active relation with the whole system. Technicality is a
> characteristic of the functional whole that covers the world
> and in which the object becomes meaningful, plays a role
> with other objects. (2014, 82)

The technical object thus does not make for a relevant scale of analysis; its coherence, its technicality, can only be understood through the examination of the network it is but a node of. Isolating the machine makes it meaningless. That technical network is, to Simondon, immediately geographical—and, as you may already have sensed, potentially endless. It covers the whole world. Simondon's conception of technicality as a network has led him to develop a concern for the modes of interaction between these networks and the social and physical geography in which they are inscribed. His later texts show the emergence of the environmental question, but also of a possible economic and cultural revaluation, through technical means, of the "most underprivileged places"—the countryside or the mountains, among others. Thus, he wrote, "a sort of reversal of civilization would be achievable through the redesign of networks" (2014, 440).

Thinking media apparatuses in terms of technical networks forces us to include within "media" the geography of infrastructures that constitute the basis of these networks. In particular, electricity comes to the fore as an essential precondition for (almost) any possible media flow. Projectors, cameras, editing or processing machines, television or radio receivers, smartphones, etc., all need electricity, at least since the generalization of talking pictures. As we have seen, electric generators are a fundamental element of any equipment system, as long as autonomy is aimed at: they were part of Jean Rouch's Super 8 kits in Mozambique, as well as of the mobile vans given by the USSR. That was already the case from the 1920s on in rural parts of Europe, where in most places cinema arrived before electricity. Itinerant projectionists, or priests, or school teachers aiming at an occasional elevating event, had to buy or rent an electrical generator together with the projector and film prints.

In 1979, Armand Mattelart described Mozambique as "a country where one of the technical obstacles for the expansion of the mass communication network is the shortage of pencils, of marker pens for wall newspapers, and of batteries for transistor radios" (1979, 494). Debra Spitulnik has shown, in "Mobile Machines and Fluid Audiences," how radio culture in Zambia was in many ways polarized by the availability—or lack thereof—of sources of electricity (2002). The radio had different modes of presence in electrified urban neighborhoods, and in rural areas, where batteries, quite expensive items, were the only possible source. These places thus saw the growth of a specific technical culture focused on the preservation of battery life. There is a cultural geography of radio in Zambia that is strongly connected with the technical geography of the electrical network.

At the beginning of his 2016 book on Nollywood, Haynes recalled that the legendary Nigerian electrical problems, with breakdowns occurring repeatedly even in the largest cities, had become the symbol of the failure of national politics (xv). Confronted with this situation, inhabitants found informal solutions: they multiplied pirate connections—which in turn strained the network—while companies had to create their own energetic infrastructures. Of course this structure involves video production companies, and is not unrelated with the very shape that the Nollywood industry has taken.

The question of electricity, of generators and battery life, also shows how the technical network appears as the relevant scale to question the environmental impact of technologies. Indeed, batteries are integral to the presence of radios within the local ecological system, in the same way as chemical laboratories are to the analogue film system, or coltan mines in the Democratic Republic of Congo to the iPhone environmental balance sheet.

The notion of technical network is key to understanding the problems raised in 1978 Mozambique. What all the participants aimed at, though probably Rouch and the Film Institute in particular, was first and foremost to create a complete and autonomous technical network within the country, which would be rid of any connection with the formerly colonizing or contemporary imperialist countries. Undoubtedly, the basic machines would have to be imported, either from the United States, Europe, or Japan, as they could not be made in the local industry. But once they were here, they were meant to become part of a network that was working and sustainable entirely on the local level, with a complete independence from their countries of origin. All the operations of use and maintenance had to be feasible in the country, all the infrastructures, facilities, tools, skills, and knowledge, were meant to be available here. That is why for Rouch the Kodak Supermatic 8 processor was the decisive element: with it, it became possible to imagine moving the entirety of the film technical network—production as well as distribution, with know-how included—within any African country, with almost complete autonomy. Thinking in terms of technical network was in this case more important than the aesthetic aspect, because it was there—for Rouch anyway—that the geopolitical aspect of technology massively crystallized.

6. Format Geographies, Standard Politics

As explained by Simondon, the technical object in its industrial phase is necessarily part of a network first in the sense that it is made of spare parts, which must be repairable and exchangeable. This supposes their standardization. The construction of these technical networks thus involves the establishment of standards allowing for the interoperability of apparatuses and the circulation of productions. In the film and media world, these standards materialize among other things in the creation of formats. Jonathan Sterne has analyzed the "meaning" of the MP3 format regarding the contemporary transformations of the music industry as well as of the listening experience. In this framework, he studied both its technical constitution as a *format*, based on the "perceptual coding" of sound, and the political implications of its institution as a *standard*:

48   Standards simultaneously engage technical and political
      problems.… A particular standard is situated among
      technical, industrial, and aesthetic concerns all at once—
      and attempts to negotiate them. [MP3 thus became] an
      emergent, crystallized set of understandings, practices,
      protocols, and industrial relationships. The standard allowed
      for the proliferation of standard objects that could move
      between countries, media, operating systems, and protocols.
      (2012, 129, 144, 146)

Media technical networks are first and foremost networks of
interoperability and compatibility. This entails in return, as we
have seen with Mosse's work, the creation of incompatibilities.
The networks' designs circumscribe spaces of rejection,
peripheries maintained in the outside. They oppose free flow
regions—'free' as in 'free trade agreements'—to unattainable
places. In the analogue film world, there was absolutely no interoperability across the various film formats. A 35mm print could
not be played through a 16mm projector, nor vice versa. There
existed hybrid machines, but they remained rare and complicated to handle. Formats were technically basically incompatible.
From that perspective, the borders between formats were no
less sealed than those between media. VHS could not be played
in a European "cinema"; but neither could Super 8. Standardized formats were thus deployed in hermetically closed sets
of machines and productions, which then came to occupy very
different places within cultures. The 35mm format meant feature
films, centralized commercial production and distribution,
the movie theater. 16mm denoted first the amateur context,
but soon educational and useful cinema, distributed through
parallel and sometimes non-commercial networks, like univer-
sities, museums, churches, mobile projection units, etc. These
two networks were completely independent from one another.
For certain filmmakers, the gradual disappearance of 16mm
projectors during the decades preceding the digital turn meant

that some of their works became invisible, if not their entire production.

Questions of culture and geography are immediately inscribed in this technical separation of circulation networks through distribution formats. For instance, cinema has long been perceived as an essentially urban phenomenon—a representation that film studies have largely contributed to strengthening. *Cinema* never really was. But *35mm cinema* was indeed essentially an urban phenomenon. In Mozambique, as in Canada and many other places, the cinema accessible outside of the big cities was mostly 16mm film. That meant different perceptual characteristics, but that could also mean that cinema in these rural areas would not be associated at all with entertainment, fiction, or stars; rather with education, political or religious propaganda, social work, etc. Technical networks are not only material in the strictest sense; as networks of interoperability (and exclusions), they shape the circulation of objects, and construct as well as are constructed by the modes of presence of the media in culture. They therefore prove relevant beyond the technical level, and show levels of coherence that may be at least as strong as that of the medium. They also immediately involve the geographical level. That is true for film, but also for television. In a 1954 text, Gilbert Simondon proposed creating a "rural educational television network" in France. Its possibility was to him connected with maintaining the "lower" 441-line format, then about to be abandoned in favor of the 625-line SECAM standard:

> The primitive 441-line standard, which is rejected by the urban civilization, is wonderfully appropriate to the educational needs of rural areas: the urban infirmities of the 441-line format (an extreme sensitivity to the interferences provoked by car engines ...) disappear in the rural context, whereas the great quality of transmission in the low bands fully materializes: the narrowness of the bandwidth ... allows for the use of a carrier whose frequency is low enough for long distance propagation (150 km) to become possible with

low power and much cheaper equipment for emission as well as reception. Using the 441-line standard in the French countryside means ensuring the possibility of *departmental centers of television news*. France must keep these two standards, with their appropriate means, if it wants the rural civilization to develop equally with urban civilization. (2014, 238)

Of course this didn't happen. Standards do not appreciate sharing the field. A somewhat similar proposal came up again in France in 2006, in an official report for the Centre national du cinéma et de l'image animée entitled *Goodbye to celluloid? The challenges of digital projection*. Only a few months after the publication of the DCI "D-cinema" specifications, its author Daniel Goudineau proposed establishing another standard, to be called "E-cinema"—"E" for "Electronic." It would be connected with the creation of a network of "lightweight digital" film theaters. These would not try to comply with the "D-cinema" specifications, perceived as too expensive and too strongly connected with the US production and criteria. These theaters would purchase cheaper equipment, and ideally, according to Goudineau, would restrict their programs to the films which had themselves no budget for "2K" shooting—art films, documentaries, etc. They could, however, also present substandard versions of traditional films, given that their screen sizes were often limited—in the case of rural theaters for instance (2006, 23–24). As was discussed in Mozambique by Ruy Guerra, however, this meant that rural—or African—spectators would only have access to a "substandard" film experience...

In any case, again, this didn't happen. D-cinema rules, and the sun never sets on its empire. The format police were there to make sure to replicate in the digital media reign the extraordinary industrial success of 35mm—a universal standard, playable in each movie theater everywhere on the planet, and stable to the point of being basically the same since 1889, and having never been modified since 1928. In fact, the situation couldn't be exactly reproduced, as low formats—like the files that circulate on YouTube—are below the control of the institutions in charge of standard policies. But in the controlled space of movie theaters, they saw no reason to accept the coexistence of another standard, which would institutionalize the existence of *another cinema*.

7. A Conclusion

Formats, norms, and standards dislocate media. They reveal the notion of "medium" as too wide and too abstract to describe specific "configurations of film." These are rather materialized in *technical networks*, which determine and are determined by local material cultures, local modes of representations, and the local physical environment, whether human or nonhuman. Indeed, media machines are organized by a specific topology. As private objects, owned and manipulated, they seem to relate only to the user's body, their surface acting as an intimate interface, beautifully arranged by that discipline named industrial design. But beneath that surface, mechanisms and processes constantly connect every machine with wide, global, maybe infinite networks. Those networks are best delineated through the arrangement of formats, norms, and standards that they mobilize. Taking these networks as the basis of analysis, instead of either the medium or the isolated technical object, directly inscribes media systems within a specific place and space. Technical networks are geographical as extended and as localized phenomena. The interaction of technical objects with the natural and social environment, their ecological impact, can only be understood at the network level. And in fact, the cultural coherence attributed to media should rather be searched for on the level determined by each "standard."

As geographically rooted while based on global infrastructures, technical networks always involve displacements. Media may flow, but formats, networks, are displaced. Flows seem immaterial, diaphanous, while their circulation is in fact organized by precise material conditions, commercial decisions, political aspirations, existing infrastructures, history, climate, etc. Establishing technical networks using formats and standards as a material basis helps us uncover new structures within media. In fact, media should be thought of in terms of use, rather than of reception: formats show how the uses of cinema have always been deeply diverse, and socially structured as such. "Use" is of course a technological concept, which explains the wider cultural relevance of media technical networks. Approaching media in terms of technical networks and their displacements allows us to elaborate on their geopolitical implications. "Low" formats, for instance, may still appear as "cheap" or "poor," but they may also appear as opportunities for decolonizing and decentralizing film. The question then is to understand what we actually mean by "low," "cheap," or "poor" with regard to images and sounds. We may then need to displace also ourselves in front of these works, and find decentralized aesthetic criteria, remembering that there is no such thing as unformatted media.

References

Adesanya, Afolabi. 2000. "From Film to Video." In *Nigerian Video Films*, edited by Jonathan Haynes, 37–50. Athens: Ohio University Center for International Studies.

Akrich, Madeleine. 1992. "The De-Scription of Technical Objects." In *Shaping Technology/Building Society: Studies in Sociotechnical Change*, edited by Wiebe E. Bijker and John Law, 205–224. Cambridge, MA: MIT Press.

Alencar, Miguel, Jacques d'Arthuys, Philippe Costantini, Françoise Foucault, Anna Glogowski, and Nadine Wanono. 1991. *Moçambique Super 8 1978: Histoire des seize films réalisés de juin à septembre 1978 dans le cadre des Ateliers Super 8 de l'Université de Maputo au Mozambique*. Paris: unpublished (Ateliers Varan archives).

Barrot, Pierre, ed. 2005. *Nollywood: Le Phénomène Vidéo au Nigéria*. Paris: L'Harmattan.

Bousquet, Antoine. 2018. *The Eye of War: Military Perception from the Telescope to the Drone*. Minneapolis: University of Minnesota Press.

Diawara, Manthia. 1992. *African Cinema: Politics and Culture*. Bloomington: Indiana University Press.

Digital Cinema Initiatives, LLC. 2004. "DCI Completes Overall System Requirements and Specifications for Digital Cinema." *SMPTE Motion Imaging Journal* 113 (10–11): 383.

—. 2005. "Digital Cinema Initiatives (DCI) announces final overall system requirements and specifications for digital cinema." *dcimovies.com*. Accessed October 16, 2019. https://www.dcimovies.com/press/07-27-05.html.

—. 2018. *Digital Cinema System Specification*: *Version 1.3*. *dcimovies.com*. Accessed October 16, 2019. http://dcimovies.com/specification/DCI_DCSS_Ver1-3_2018-0627.pdf.

Godard, Jean-Luc. 1979. "Rapport sur le voyage n° 2A de la société Sonimage au Mozambique." *Cahiers du Cinéma* 300: 79–129.

Goudineau, Daniel. 2006. *Adieu à la pellicule? Les enjeux de la projection numérique*. *cnc.fr*. Accessed December 19, 2018. https://www.cnc.fr/documents/36995/156431/rapport+de+Daniel+Goudineau+Adieu+à+la+pellicule++Les+enjeux+de+la+projection+numérique.pdf/e4e5257d-0e33-cb46-90a6-9186d4c9d96b.

Haynes, Jonathan. 2016. *Nollywood: The Creation of Nigerian Film Genres*. Chicago: University of Chicago Press, 2016.

Ihde, Don. 1990. *Technology and the Life World: From Garden to Earth*. Bloomington: Indiana University Press.

Joselit, David. 2013. *After Art*. Princeton, NJ: Princeton University Press.

Larkin, Brian. 2004. "Degraded Images, Distorted Sounds: Nigerian Video and the Infrastructure of Piracy." *Public Culture* 16 (2): 289–314.

Lobato, Ramon. 2012. *Shadow Economies of Cinema: Mapping Informal Film Distribution*. London: BFI.

Mattelart, Armand. 1979. "Mozambique: Communication et transition au socialisme." *Revue Tiers-Monde* 20 (79): 487–502.

Mosse, Richard. 2017. "Incoming: Text." *richardmosse.com*. Accessed December 12, 2018. http://www.richardmosse.com/projects/incoming.

Museum für Moderne Kunst, MMK. 2018. "Extreme. Nomads." *mmk.art*. Accessed October 16, 2019. https://www.mmk.art/en/whats-on/extreme-nomads/.

Ogundele, Wole. 2000. "From Folk Opera to Soap Opera: Improvisations and Transformations in Yoruba Popular Theater." In *Nigerian Video Films*, edited by Jonathan Haynes, 89–130. Athens: Ohio University Center for International Studies.

Okome, Onookome. 2010. "Nollywood & Its Critics." In *Viewing African Cinema in the Twenty First Century: Art Films and the Video Revolution*, edited by Mahir Şaul and Ralph A. Austen, 26–41. Athens: Ohio University Press.

Oudart, Jean-Pierre, and Dominique Terres. 1979. "Une expérience de Super 8 au Mozambique." *Cahiers du cinéma* 296: 54–59.

Parks, Lisa, and Nicole Starosielski. 2015. *Signal Traffic: Critical Studies of Media Infrastructures*. Urbana: University of Illinois Press.

Rouch, Jean. 1982. "Comment filmer la liberté? Entretien par Pierre Haffner." *CinémAction* 17: 15–34.

54 Simondon, Gilbert. 2014. *Sur La Technique (1953–1983)*. Paris: Presses Universitaires de France.

Spitulnik, Debra. 2002. "Mobile Machines and Fluid Audiences: Rethinking Reception Through Zambian Radio Culture." In *Media Worlds: Anthropology on New Terrain*, edited by Faye Ginsburg, Lila Abu-Lughod, and Brian Larkin, 337–354. Berkeley: University of California Press.

Sterne, Jonathan. 2012. *Mp3: The Meaning of a Format*. Durham, NC: Duke University Press.

Summers, David. 2003. *Real Spaces: World Art History and the Rise of Western Modernism*. London: Phaidon.

Unesco Institute for Statistics. 2016a. *Diversity and the Film Industry: An Analysis of the 2014 UIS Survey on Feature Film Statistics. uis.unesco.org*. Accessed December 19, 2018.

—. 2016b. "Record Number of Films Produced." *uis.unesco.org*. Accessed December 19, 2018. http://uis.unesco.org/en/news/record-number-films-produced. https://fr.unesco.org/creativity/sites/creativity/files/diversity_and_the_film_industry_2016-en.pdf.

Wasson, Haidee. 2015. "Formatting Film Studies." *Film Studies* 12: 57–61.

Wiesing, Lambert. 2010. *Artificial Presence: Philosophical Studies in Image Theory*. Stanford, CA: Stanford University Press.